BIOLOGY
in Your Everyday Life

REAL WORLD SCIENCE

E Enslow Publishing
101 W. 23rd Street
Suite 240
New York, NY 10011
USA
enslow.com

Donna M. Bozzone, Ph.D.

Published in 2020 by Enslow Publishing, LLC.
101 W. 23rd Street, Suite 240, New York, NY 10011

Copyright © 2020 by Enslow Publishing, LLC.

All rights reserved.

No part of this book may be reproduced by any means without the written permission of the publisher.

Library of Congress Cataloging-in-Publication Data

Names: Bozzone, Donna M., author.
Title: Biology in your everyday life / Donna M. Bozzone, Ph.D.
Description: New York : Enslow Publishing, 2020. | Series: Real world science
Audience: Grades 5-8. | Includes bibliographical references and index.
Identifiers: LCCN 2018042806| ISBN 9781978507630 (library bound) | ISBN 9781978509436 (paperback)
Subjects: LCSH: Biology—Juvenile literature.
Classification: LCC QH309.2 .B69 2020 | DDC 570—dc23
LC record available at https://lccn.loc.gov/2018042806

Printed in the United States of America

To Our Readers: We have done our best to make sure all website addresses in this book were active and appropriate when we went to press. However, the author and the publisher have no control over and assume no liability for the material available on those websites or on any websites they may link to. Any comments or suggestions can be sent by email to customerservice@enslow.com.

Photo Credits: Cover, p. 1 Lapina/Shutterstock.com; cover, p. 1 (science icons), back cover pattern kotoffei/Shutterstock.com; cover, p. 1 (globe graphic) Elkersh/Shutterstock.com; cover, interior pages (circular pattern) John_Dakapu/Shutterstock.com; p. 5 Budimir Jevtic/Shutterstock.com; p. 8 cigdem/Shutterstock.com; p. 10 Orchid24/Shutterstock.com; p. 11 Kateryna Kon/Shutterstock.com; p. 13 © iStockphoto.com/Syldavia; p. 18 CP DC Press/Shutterstock .com; p. 20 Soleil Nordic/Shutterstock.com; p. 23 Victor Josan/Shutterstock.com; p. 29 Tefi/Shutterstock.com; p. 30 Andy Lyons/Getty Images; p. 33 Christos Georghiou/Shutterstock.com; p. 38 Life science/Shutterstock.com; p. 40 Singkham/Shutterstock.com; p. 42 Designua/Shutterstock.com; p. 46 LightField Studios/Shutterstock.com; p. 47 margouillat photo/Shutterstock.com; p. 49 Black creator/Shutterstock.com; pp. 50-51 Andrei Minsk/Shutterstock.com.

Contents

Introduction 4

■ **Chapter 1**
The Biology of Acne 7

■ **Chapter 2**
The Biology of Sexual Development 17

■ **Chapter 3**
The Biology of the Brain 28

■ **Chapter 4**
The Biology of Energy 37

■ **Chapter 5**
The Biology of Human Differences 45

Chapter Notes 56
Glossary 59
Further Reading 61
Index 63

Introduction

Biology impacts every aspect of your life, both big and small. You, like other organisms, were born because of biological events. You grew and developed from the infant you once were because of biology. Biological mechanisms account for how your body functions, or in some cases, doesn't. The way your body responds to the foods you eat, the ways you move, and any injuries or diseases you may experience are all influenced by biology. From the moment we're born to the day we die, biology is the foundation for our lives.

The importance of biology in your everyday life as it relates to your individual body is just part of the story. Biology also impacts the environment in which we live. After all, we are not the only organisms living on this planet. How does what we do affect the well-being of other species and the balance of life in our world? When we take care of the environment by preserving the habitats where plants and animals live, nature thrives. When we pollute and spoil the quality of air, water, and soil, it does not. All of this is biology, too.

This book examines the role of biology in your everyday life by focusing on specific topics that capture experiences that you, or people you know, may encounter. First, we will consider the biological explanation for acne, as well as some possible remedies for this skin condition. Next, we will explore the biology that lies behind sex development. Third, we will turn our attention to the biological consequences of concussions, a type of brain injury that is unfortunately not all that uncommon. Fourth, we will look at how

Introduction

Biologists study all types of living organisms including bacteria, plants (shown here), and animals like humans.

our bodies get the energy we need to live. Finally, we will look at how our individual biological makeups contribute to our personal responses, like why some of us are lactose intolerant while some of us are not.

Biology in Your Everyday Life

These examples are just a sampling among the countless number of ways that biology affects what you can do, who you are, and even how you feel. Biology is indeed the science of life and therefore touches everything in your life, either directly or through some connection.

The Biology of Acne

Most people will have a pimple at some point in their lives. The occasional pimple here and there is natural; it's part of life. Clusters of pimples that are painful and won't go away, however, is something else entirely. More concerning than simple blemishes, acne affects most females and males. Its causes are complex and can result in permanent scarring of the skin. When over-the-counter creams and medications don't work, people often visit a dermatologist, a physician who specializes in skin.

Dermatologists perform thorough examinations and will often prescribe stronger medications, like Accutane or minocycline, to treat acne. With the proper treatment, acne can be managed and, for some, disappear completely.

How does acne develop and why do some people get it while others don't? Are there ways to reduce the likelihood of having your skin break out? Why do medications like Accutane and minocycline work?

Skin—Your Body's Biggest Organ

All organisms are either cells or are composed of cells. Thus, cells are the basic units of life.

Sometimes the cells in the body function as individuals. For example, the white blood cells of the immune system crawl around the body seeking invaders, like bacteria. Once white blood cells encounter these uninvited guests, the cells eat the bacteria and, as a result, prevent infection. More often, the cells of the body organize to form more complicated structures: tissues, organs, and

Biology in Your Everyday Life

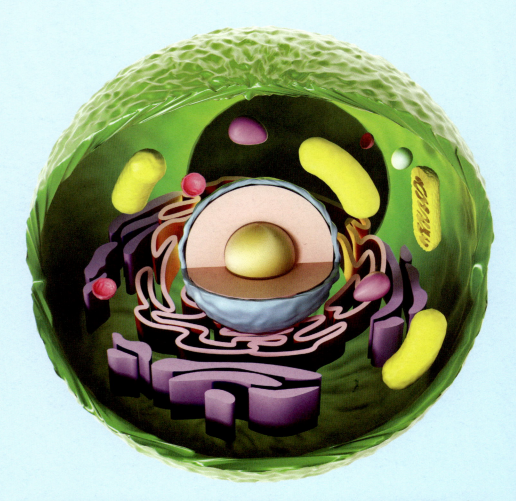

Cells are small but complex, possessing internal organelles that take care of the cell's functions.

organ systems. Tissues are a group of cells that are attached to each other to carry out a specific function. Organs are composed of tissues that share a common function. Similarly, organisms with a shared overall objective form an organ system. For example, blood moves in the body thanks to cardiac muscle, which is a type of tissue found in the heart, which is itself an organ in the circulatory system.

Skin is the outer covering of the body. Composed of many layers, skin serves several functions: it protects us from infection; it prevents the excessive loss of water from the body; it keeps us warm by insulating the body; it allows us to sense the environment through temperature, touch, and other sensations; it protects muscle, bones, and organs; and it even synthesizes Vitamin D, a nutrient necessary for healthy bones. Depending on its location on the body, skin may be hairy, as seen on our heads, or hairless, like on the palms of our hands.

Acne

With more than six hundred million people affected, acne is the eighth most common disease worldwide.[1] More than 80 percent of teenagers experience acne to some degree.[2] In fact, this skin condition can appear in childhood. A study of 365 nine- to ten-year-old girls revealed that 78 percent of them had signs of acne.[3]

Acne can be mild, moderate, or severe. The blemishes that occur are all due to the plugging of hair follicles with oil and dead skin cells. Hair follicles are the microscopic openings in the skin from which hair grows. Acne can only appear on skin that has hair. This is why you will never see pimples on the palms of hands or the soles of feet. Whiteheads refer to clogged pores that are closed, whereas blackheads are clogged open pores. Pores are tiny openings in the skin from which oil or sweat is released. Pimples, raised red bumps with white tips, form when clogged pores become inflamed and infected. In the most serious forms of acne, nodules form under the skin. Nodules are solid, painful lumps. Severe cases of acne can lead to permanent scarring.

Biology in Your Everyday Life

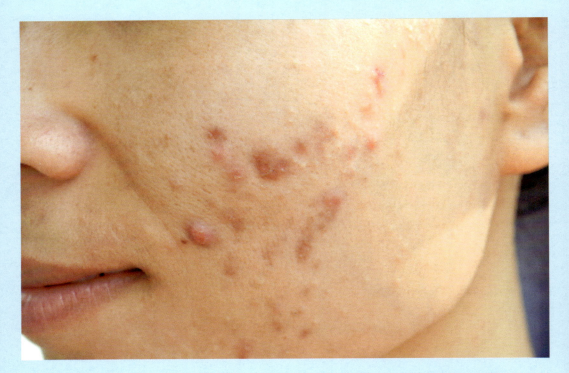

While not too severe, the acne shown here may need medical attention to treat it.

Accutane is a drug that reduces the production of sebum, an oily substance that is secreted by the sebaceous or oil glands of the skin. Minocycline is an antibiotic that is used to kill the bacterium *Propionibacterium acnes*.

P. acnes are found on oily skin. These bacteria can actually change the way skin develops resulting in the formation of inflamed nodules or bumps.

Accutane and minocycline are successful treatments because both of these drugs are lipid, or fat, soluble. This means they will dissolve in lipids just as readily as olive oil and corn oil will mix

The Biology of Acne

together. Once the drugs enter an individual's bloodstream, they can easily pass through the cell membranes of both *P. acnes* and the individual's own cells. All bacteria and human cells are enclosed by a membrane that is rich in lipids. Cell membranes are essential structures in cells because they regulate everything that enters and leaves cells as well as how cells communicate with each other.

Risk Factors for Acne

Whether or not a person will develop acne depends mostly on genetics. If one or both parents struggled with acne when they were younger, it increases the likelihood that their children

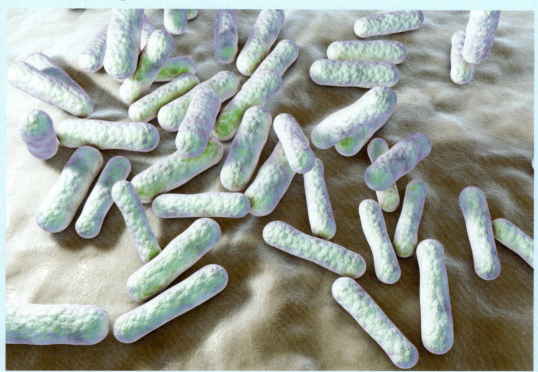

The bacterium *P. acnes* can live on the skin without producing problems, but in some cases it causes acne.

Biology in Your Everyday Life

will, too. Therefore, family history is probably the biggest risk factor. Fortunately, most acne is not the severe form.

The second biggest risk factor is adolescence. The hormonal changes that occur during puberty can increase oil production in the skin. While eating greasy foods neither causes nor worsens acne, working in an area where there is a lot of grease or oil present, such as near a fry vat, can clog pores and worsen acne. Some foods do worsen acne, however. Eating foods that are rich in refined carbohydrates can led to blemishes. Such foods include cake, cookies, candy, and white bread.

Some other factors also influence whether or not someone will develop acne. For instance, friction or pressure on the skin

Myths About Acne

Because acne is generally so visible, many people who have it feel self-conscious around others. Individuals without acne worry that they might get it and wonder how to avoid it. All of this anxiety inevitably results in myths about acne. Here are a few claims that are simply untrue:

- Eating greasy food causes acne. *It doesn't.*
- Using cosmetics or make-up will cause or worsen acne. *If you use oil-free make-up and wash it off every day, there is no effect on acne.*
- Acne is caused by dirty skin and poor hygiene. *No, it isn't.*

The Biology of Acne

Some skin creams can help reduce and prevent further outbreaks of acne.

can lead to a break out. For this reason, it is good to avoid tight clothing or backpack straps that rub or pinch. Stress can also make acne worse, which is especially vexing since having a breakout can be a source of stress.

Biology in Your Everyday Life

Treatments and Prevention

Before visiting a dermatologist, people often try some self-care remedies to treat their acne. Sometimes using mild soap to avoid irritating the skin or taking over-the-counter treatments, like benzoyl peroxide, can be helpful. It is also important to maintain good skin hygiene by eating well, drinking water, and showering regularly.

Self-care is effective for many, but not all, people with acne. If these efforts don't work, the next step is to see a dermatologist who can prescribe stronger medication. For most people, acne clears up at the end of adolescence.

Activity: Transport of Water Across a Membrane

Cell membranes regulate everything that enters and leaves cells, including water. Use deshelled chicken eggs to simulate "giant cells" and study osmosis, the movement of water across their membranes.

Things You Will Need:

- Two chicken eggs
- Plastic cups
- Plastic wrap
- White vinegar
- Pancake syrup
- String
- Ruler

If you have a scale, measure the weights of the deshelled eggs before and after the experiment.

■ 1. Place two chicken eggs in individual plastic cups and cover them with white vinegar. Cover the tops of the cups with plastic wrap. Let them sit overnight.

■ 2. Remove the vinegar and replace it with fresh vinegar. Let the eggs soak another twenty-four hours.

■ 3. Take the deshelled eggs and wipe them gently with a paper towel (they are fragile without their shells). Measure the eggs' circumferences along their long axes by carefully wrapping a string around the eggs like a belt. Measure the length of the string that encircles the eggs. Record your data.

Biology in Your Everyday Life

■ **4.** Repeat step #3 except measure the short axes of the eggs. Record your data.

■ **5.** Gently place one egg in a cup and cover it with water. Let it sit overnight.

■ **6.** Gently place the other egg in a cup with pancake syrup. Let it sit overnight.

■ **7.** Remove the egg from the water and very carefully measure the circumference of the long and short axes of the egg. Record your data.

■ **8.** Repeat step # 7 with the egg in syrup.

■ **9.** Compare the sizes (and weights, if you had a scale) of the eggs after sitting in water or syrup with the sizes at the start of your experiment. What do you observe? How do you explain the results?

The Biology of Sexual Development

Chapter 2

Running on the dirt roads of Limpopo, South Africa, Caster Semenya dreamed of being a champion. In 2008, Semenya participated in her first international track and field events, winning gold medals in two major track and field competitions. In fact, Semenya's performance was so spectacular that she qualified for the 2009 World Championship in Berlin. Eighteen-year-old Semenya appeared to be on top of her game—a world-class athlete with a bright future.

But then the rumors began to surface. Some doubted that Semenya was actually a woman. They said she looked masculine and performed so much better than her competitors that she must be male. Semenya was subjected to two rounds of tests to see if she was female; the first was in Pretoria, South Africa, and the second was in Berlin, Germany, a day before her race.

Even though the tests showed that Semenya was female, the rumors did not stop. In many ways, the situation actually got worse. After she ran successfully in the semifinal round, a TV reporter outside of the stadium accused her of being a man. Although visibly upset, Semenya managed to win the world championship anyway.

The International Association of Athletics Foundations (IAAF), an organization that enforces rules in competitive sports, broke its own confidentiality rules and leaked the information about the medical tests. Worse, a newspaper in Australia claimed that test results showed that Semenya had external female genitals but no ovaries or uterus. The tabloid also claimed that she had undescended testes, male sex organs, and levels of the hormone

Biology in Your Everyday Life

Shown running in the 800-meter race in the 2016 Olympics, Caster Semenya went on to win the gold medal.

The Biology of Sexual Development

testosterone that are three times higher than those of an average woman (but much lower than a man's). While we don't know if these reports are accurate (the tests are supposed to be private), we do know that Semenya was raised as a girl and sees herself as female. Suddenly, at the age of eighteen, the world was telling her otherwise.

Caster Semenya returned to the University of Pretoria, her athletic future uncertain. The IAAF allowed her to keep her gold medals because she did not commit fraud by competing as a woman. However, Semenya did not run competitively with women in international track and field competitions for almost a year as she waited for the IAAF's decision regarding her eligibility. Finally, Semenya got some good news when, in 2010, they declared that she was free to compete professionally with other female athletes.[1] She won a silver medal in the 800 meters at both the 2011 world championships and the 2012 Summer Olympics in London. But the IAAF had a huge problem. It posed a very difficult question: what is the ultimate difference between males and females? Is there something that can be measured or tested that can show that someone is a man or a woman? Or might there be still other outcomes to sexual development?

How Do Males and Females Form?

When a baby is born, one of the first questions everyone asks is whether it is a boy or a girl. However, not everyone falls clearly into one of the two categories. Is it even the case that there are only two categories of sex—male and female? Some scientists estimate that as much as 1.7 percent of the population has what many physicians call a disorder of sexual development (DSD).[2] Others suggest that variation in sexual development is not actually disordered, simply different from what is often expected

Biology in Your Everyday Life

and sometimes very different from the standard definitions of female and male. Some individuals even go through life never knowing they have a developmental difference. To understand this variability, we need to know how males and females form.

The Stages of Sex Development

In humans and other mammals, the first set of instructions for sexual development is found on the sex chromosomes. Humans have two types of sex chromosomes, X and Y. Chromosomes are structures in cells that contain genes or inherited materials. Typically, males are XY and females are XX. When gametes, or sex cells, are produced for reproduction, males make sperm that have an X chromosome or a Y chromosome. Females make eggs that have an X chromosome. When the egg and sperm fuse together during fertilization, the resulting embryo will get an X from the mother and an X or Y from the father.

So far this seems pretty straightforward: XX usually means that the embryo will develop into a girl, and XY means that a boy

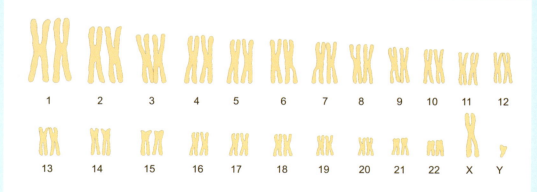

Each human typically has forty-six chromosomes. Of them, two are sex chromosomes, either XX or XY.

The Biology of Sexual Development

will most likely form. Girls have female sex organs in the form of ovaries. Boys have male sex organs called testes. However, chromosomes provide just the first piece of information in sexual development. They're responsible for whether ovaries or testes form. But ovaries or testes do not necessarily produce a specific sex in an individual.

In addition to ovaries and testes, there are other sex-related body characteristics. Usually, men have external genitals, or sex organs. Women, on the other hand, generally have breasts, a uterus (or womb), and a vagina. Men and women also differ in the structure of their pelvic bones or hipbones, voice tones, and the locations of their body fat and hair. Chemical signals called hormones are responsible for these characteristics.

Chromosome Instructions

Until an embryo is six weeks old, it is not possible to tell whether it is male or female by its appearance. However, structures that will eventually become ovaries or testes are already present in the lower abdomen, awaiting instructions from specific genes.

Even these instructions are more than just XX in females versus XY in males. Ordinarily, the Y chromosome has a particular gene called SRY, which is required for the development of testes. If SRY is not working properly, even though the embryo is XY, ovaries develop. If an XX embryo has the SRY gene because of a genetic mistake, testes develop.

The sex characteristics regulated by hormones develop in several stages—in the embryo, in fetal development, and during puberty. Until at least the seventh week of development, embryos, whether XY or XX, have the internal parts of *both* sexes. These parts are set of tubes and ducts—the Wolffian ducts and the Müllerian ducts. XX embryos eventually lose the Wolffian ducts

Biology in Your Everyday Life

and keep the Müllerian. In XY embryos, however, it is the other way around. They lose the Müllerian and keep the Wolffian ducts.

Hormone Instructions

In XY embryos, the testes secrete two critical hormones: anti-Müllerian hormone and testosterone. Anti-Müllerian hormone triggers the destruction of Müllerian ducts. Testosterone promotes the development of Wolffian ducts and the penis. Testosterone also inhibits breast formation and regulates the descent of testes into a pouch called the scrotum. Testes are able to move toward or away from the body throughout a man's life. For example, testes will move closer to the body when it is cold.

In XX embryos, ovaries release the hormone estrogen, which promotes the development of the Müllerian ducts, oviducts (the passageway from the ovaries to the uterus), the uterus, and the upper end of the vagina. Ovaries also make some testosterone, just not as much as testes do.

External genitals do not start out looking male or female either. At six weeks, the embryo has a small bud between its legs. Eventually, it will form either a penis or clitoris. By nine weeks, there are two swellings on either side of a groove between the legs. By fourteen weeks, this groove has typically disappeared in male embryos, and the scrotum has formed from the swellings. In females, the groove generally becomes the opening of the vagina, and the swelling becomes other folds of the female genitals called the labia majora and labia minora. Amazingly, all these changes are regulated by hormones. That is why most babies are often easy to label male or female at birth.

The final body changes come with puberty, due to a dramatic increase in sex hormones. These changes make the differences between males and females even more obvious—most of the time.

The Biology of Sexual Development

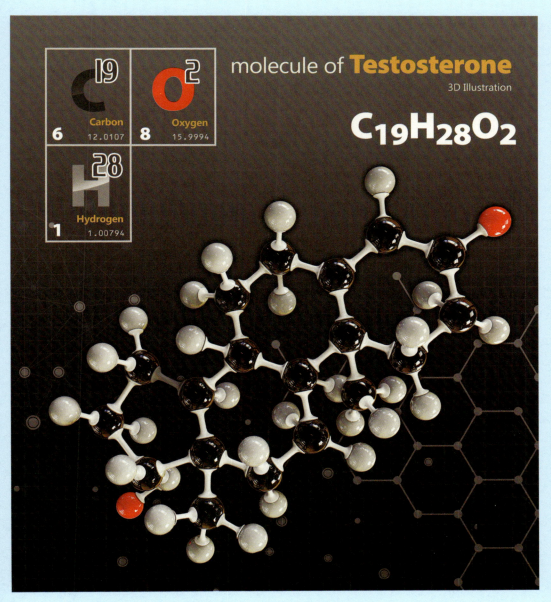

Often called a male sex hormone, testosterone is actually made by both males and females.

Biology in Your Everyday Life

What Happens if the Hormonal Signals Are Missing or Misread?

In almost 2 percent of men and women, however, events play out differently. In fact, there are more than forty different types of disorders of sex development (DSD).[3] One dramatic example is androgen-insensitive syndrome (AIS) in women.

In androgen-insensitivity syndrome, individuals who are XY do not develop as males because their cells are deaf to the instructions saying, "make male genitalia." More technically, they lack cell receptors that bind, or stick, to testosterone. Because AIS individuals are XY, the SRY gene functions correctly, and they develop testes. Clearly, the gene instructions work. The testes make anti-Müllerian hormone, which causes Müllerian ducts to degenerate. The testes also produce testosterone. However, without the right testosterone receptors in cells, no external male genitals form. Rather, the testes remain inside the body. And since the Müllerian ducts are destroyed, no internal female body parts form either.

As an AIS embryo develops in its mother's uterus, it is exposed to estrogen produced by the mother's ovaries. This estrogen is responsible for breast development and the female pattern of hair and fat. As a result, a person with AIS will look and be female, even though her chromosomal makeup is XY and has developed testes but no ovaries. In some cases, women are unaware they have AIS until they try to find out why they're not menstruating or why they are unable to become pregnant.

Sometimes AIS can be partial. Whispers of testosterone signals can get through if the cell receptors work partially. When this occurs, a woman may be XY and possess external female genitals, but she may also have some characteristics that are typically

Sex Testing in Sports

In the 1930s, Stella Walsh and Helen Stephens dominated women's track and field. During the 1936 Olympic Games, the press reported that both women were actually men. The Olympic Committee examined Stephens and confirmed that she had female genitals.

Rumors began spreading like wildfire. Male athletes from Eastern Europe were said to have bound their genitals in order to compete as women. To compete in the 1966 European Athletics Championship, women had to agree to a humiliating physical examination. Yet of 243 women examined, none had atypical genitals.[4]

In 1991, Olympic officials began testing for the SRY gene. At the 1996 Olympics, three thousand women were tested, and eight were positive for SRY. Of these, seven had AIS and one had a different DSD. All eight were allowed to compete.[5]

Sex testing has never revealed anyone deliberately misrepresenting his or her sex. In 1999, the Olympics Committee finally abandoned sex testing.

associated with males, such as greater muscle mass, little breast development, and a less female-shaped pelvis.

The controversy surrounding Semenya did not end in 2012. Some people argued that women like her, who naturally had high testosterone levels, enjoyed an unfair athletic advantage. The IAAF proposed that such women should take medication to lower their testosterone levels. The IAAF was brought to court in 2015; the court ruled that there was no evidence that extra testosterone naturally produced in a woman's body gave her an unfair advantage. In 2016, Semenya won an Olympic gold medal in the women's 800 meters. In 2018, the IAAF announced new rules that required women who had high testosterone and who competed in the 400m, 800m, and 1500m races to take medication to lower their testosterone levels.[6] This rule is only in effect for these specific races. Interestingly, these are the exact events in which Caster Semenya competes.

Activity: What Are the Chances of Having the Chromosomal Instructions to Make a Boy or a Girl?

Use marbles to represent eggs or sperm and see the odds of having an XX or XY embryo.

Things You Will Need:

- **Marbles (two different colors)**
- **Plastic cups**

■ **1.** Place two black marbles in a cup labeled "egg" and a black marble and a white marble in a second cup labeled "sperm."

■ **2.** Choose a marble from each cup without looking and place them in a third cup labeled "embryo." The black marble represents an X chromosome and the white one represents the Y. Record whether you have two black marbles (XX) or a black and a white one (XY).

■ **3.** Repeat steps 1 and 2 fifty times, recording the chromosome pairing for each "embryo."

■ **4.** What percentages of the embryos are XX? XY? Explain this result.

The Biology of the Brain

Imagine a hollow sphere with a ball of Jell-O inside taking up almost all of the available space. What do you suppose would happen to the Jell-O if you threw this sphere against a wall? Can you envision the Jell-O sloshing forward, hitting the inside of the sphere, and perhaps bouncing back to hit the opposite surface? This is what happens when a person suffers a concussion.

Concussions

A hard knock to the head can cause a concussion, or brain bruise. The force of the blow causes the brain to collide with the inner surface of the skull. In some cases, the collision between the brain and skull results in bleeding and the tearing of delicate nerve fibers. At its most extreme, the injury can cause dangerous brain swelling, which can produce widespread brain damage and death.

Brain injuries are relatively common. In the United States, someone suffers a serious head injury every twenty-one seconds.[1] The most common causes are falls, accidents, physical violence, and contact sports like football and hockey. Although protective headgear may help, it does not eliminate all risk of concussion.

If you receive a blow to the head that knocks you out or leaves you dazed, you are concussed. Other symptoms may include headache, nausea, amnesia, confusion, dizziness, and slurred speech. Your concussion may be obvious to those around you, or it may be more subtle. Symptoms can last for days to weeks and even longer. No matter how mild or serious the concussion,

The Biology of the Brain

Even though it is protected by the bony skull, the brain is sometimes injured or bruised.

Biology in Your Everyday Life

Concussions are a risk for athletes playing any contact sport, such as football.

it is essential to minimize further brain trauma until the injury has healed.

In sports, there is sometimes a tendency to shake it off and get back into the game even after a hard hit that causes the athlete to "see stars." This is a dangerous thing to do. The full extent of

The Connection Between Mental Health and Physical Health

Mental health disorders can be due to anything from brain injury or defects to an imbalance of the chemicals that cells in the nervous system use to communicate. One of the most common mental health issues diagnosed today is attention-deficit/hyperactivity disorder (ADHD).

In the United States, 20 percent of all boys are diagnosed with ADHD by the time they get to high school. Many of these children take Ritalin to treat it.[2] Symptoms of ADHD include forgetfulness, impulsiveness, distractibility, fidgeting, and impatience. Some cases of ADHD are due to a reduced amount of dopamine, a molecule in the nervous system. Ritalin acts by increasing the release of dopamine, thus diminishing ADHD symptoms.

Some people argue that in many cases these ADHD symptoms are simply childhood behaviors and that ADHD is overdiagnosed. Others argue that when symptoms cause problems for a child in at least two settings–school and home, for instance–the diagnosis of ADHD is appropriate.

Biology in Your Everyday Life

the injury from that initial hit might not be known for hours or perhaps days. Even after the severity of the concussion has been determined, the athlete should sit out their sport until a medical professional can confirm that the concussion has healed. This caution is essential because once a person suffers a concussion, he or she is more likely to suffer another. Athletes, and others, who suffer multiple concussions over their lives experience brain damage in a cumulative or additive way. Each concussion adds more injury to an already wounded brain. No matter how important the event, brain damage goes far beyond taking one for the team.

The Parts of the Human Brain

The average brain weighs around 3 pounds (1.3 kilograms).[3] Protected by the bones of the skull and the meninges, a durable connective tissue, the brain is organized in a modular manner as a series of units. The various modules of the brain are themselves organized into smaller components and often further divided. Brain function sometimes comes from a subsection of the brain, but it more often comes from the communication and interactions from many parts. Let's consider the major components of the brain.

Hindbrain

The hindbrain is located at the base of the skull, right above the spinal cord. The hindbrain is responsible for the control of many basic bodily functions necessary for survival. It is composed of three subunits:

- *Medulla oblongata:* influences the brain centers that regulate sleep and waking. It also helps control breathing and circulation, and it coordinates the motor responses that occur when you cough or sneeze.

The Biology of the Brain

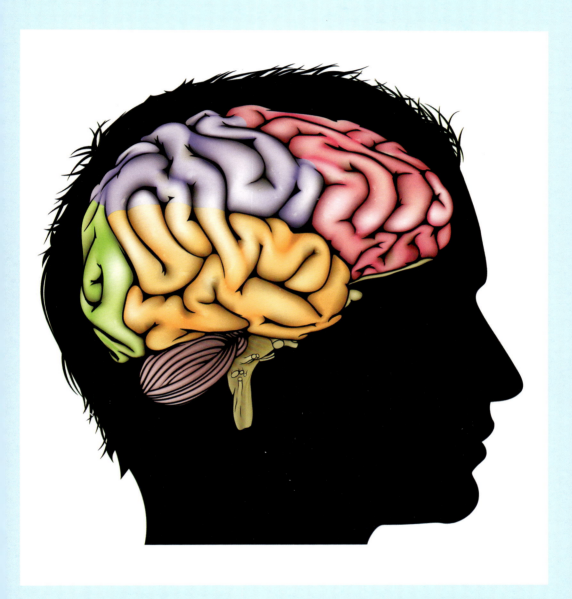

Although the entire brain works as a whole, subsections of the brain have specific functions, too.

Biology in Your Everyday Life

- *Cerebellum:* responsible for organizing what we see, hear, and feel. It coordinates movement and balance and also plays an important role in the control of the fine use of your hands and your language skills.
- *Pons:* directs the communication between the cerebellum and the forebrain. The pons also helps control breathing and circulation.

Midbrain

Along with the medulla oblongata and the pons, the midbrain forms the brainstem. All information moving to and from other brain regions passes through the brainstem, which selects what to send on. The midbrain plays an important role coordinating responses to light and sound.

Forebrain

By far the most highly developed and largest region of the brain, the forebrain is composed of the olfactory bulbs, thalamus, hypothalamus, and cerebrum:

- *Olfactory bulbs*: provide you with sensory information about smell.
- *Thalamus*: a relay switch. It sorts incoming and outgoing data.
- *Hypothalamus*: a master control center. It regulates body temperature, blood pressure, hunger, sex drive, emotions, thirst, and reactions to stress.
- *Cerebrum*: the largest and most complex component of all. Accounting for 80–85 percent of brain mass in humans,[4] the cerebrum is responsible for many of the characteristics that most people consider distinctly human: reasoning, mathematical ability, artistic ability, imagination, language, and personality. The cerebrum creates the perceptions we gather

with our senses: sight, hearing, smell, taste, and touch. Without a functioning cerebrum, people would be blind and deaf even if they had functioning eyes and ears. Similarly, tastes, odors, and physical sensations wouldn't exist without the cerebrum that allows us to experience them.

The forebrain is also home to the limbic system. Comprising parts of the cerebrum and two structures called the hippocampus and amygdala, the limbic system is in charge of physical drive and instincts. In addition, the limbic system is partly responsible for emotions, learning, and memory.

Actually, most of what we know about the relationship between specific brain structures and functions comes from scientists studying the behavior and functioning of people who have suffered brain trauma due to illness or injuries like concussions.

Activity: Taste, Smell, and Vision: Do Your Senses Interact?

See whether you can taste the difference between Skittles of different flavors and whether or not your sense of smell and/or sight helps you to taste more accurately.

Things You Will Need:

- **Skittles (regular and sour)**
- **Four bowls**
- **Blindfold**
- **Nose plugs**
- **Five or more volunteers**

■ **1.** Set up four tasting stations. In each, have a bowl containing one of the following: sweet red Skittles, sour red Skittles, sweet yellow Skittles, and sour yellow Skittles.

■ **2.** Blindfold a volunteer. Have them taste a Skittle and identify its flavor. Record the response. Repeat this for all four types of Skittles. Encourage your volunteer to drink water between taste tests.

■ **3.** Repeat this test with four or more blindfolded volunteers.

■ **4.** Repeat this test with all volunteers who are now wearing nose plugs.

■ **5.** Repeat this test with all volunteers who are both blindfolded and wearing nose plugs.

■ **6.** Repeat this test with all volunteers who are neither blindfolded, nor wearing nose plugs.

■ **7.** Is the accuracy of taste influenced by being able to see and/or smell? Explain your thoughts.

The Biology of Energy

Chapter 4

On June 6, 1822, Alexis St. Martin, a twenty-year-old who worked for the American Fur Company on Mackinac Island, Michigan, was accidentally shot in the stomach and ribs at close range with buckshot. Little did St. Martin, or anyone else, know that this terrible accident would pave the way for understanding how energy is extracted from food.

Stationed at a nearby US Army post, Dr. William Beaumont was summoned to treat St. Martin. Beaumont did not expect St. Martin to survive such a serious wound—a hole had literally been blown open in his stomach. Nevertheless, Beaumont cared for St. Martin to the best of his ability and, amazingly, the injured man recovered. However, while the edges healed, the hole in St. Martin's stomach remained open.

Dr. Beaumont saw an opportunity for an experimental analysis of digestion in St. Martin's situation. St. Martin was the subject—and laboratory—for a series of experiments carried out over the span of eleven years. The experiments fell into two categories. In one, Beaumont placed various foods into St. Martin's stomach to observe their digestion in the natural environment. In the second category, Beaumont removed gastric juices from St. Martin's stomach and incubated various foods in these juices. In this way, Beaumont was able to observe digestion outside the body.

Beaumont discovered that the digestion process was the same, regardless of whether it occurred inside an actual stomach or outside the body. The overall conclusion was clear: digestion relied upon chemicals made by the body.[1]

Biology in Your Everyday Life

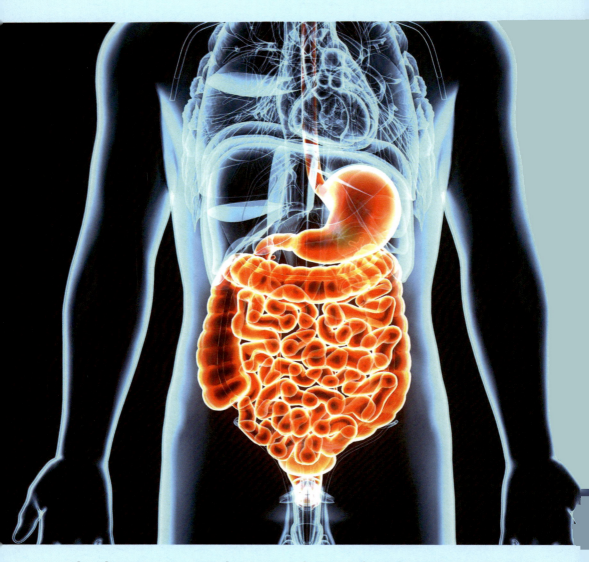

The digestive system begins at the mouth and continues through the pharynx, esophagus, stomach, small intestine, large intestine, and rectum and ends at the anus, the other opening.

How Do Cells Obtain Energy?

Life is an active process. Organisms extract energy from their environments and use this energy to function, through a process of converting or changing energy. Energy is defined as the ability to do work, which includes everything an organism does: move, make molecules, eat, reproduce, and so on. One component of understanding the biochemistry of organisms is bioenergetics, or the flow of energy through living systems. To understand bioenergetics, we must know how organisms obtain energy and how they use this energy to function, especially making complex molecules and structures like cells.

If we consider the big view of energy flow in the living world, there are two sources of energy for organisms: sunlight and food. More specifically, photosynthetic organisms capture and convert energy from sunlight into energy found in the sugar molecules they produce. Other organisms eat food and extract energy in the process of cell respiration. This extracted energy is used to power a variety of cellular, and by extension, organismal functions.

Photosynthesis

Either in a direct or indirect way, all of the energy used by most species on the planet comes from the sunlight captured by photosynthesis. Photosynthesis is a biochemical reaction that converts water and carbon dioxide into sugar. Carbon dioxide is a gas; animals, like us, release carbon dioxide every time we exhale, or breathe out. Sunlight provides the energy for the conversion. This capacity to convert solar energy to energy is what makes so many different forms of life possible. Sugar has a lot of calories, a measure of the stored energy it contains. Cells use the energy stored in sugar to perform the biochemical reactions needed for life.

Biology in Your Everyday Life

Plants capture energy from sunlight and use it to produce sugars, which then give energy to other organisms.

We can illustrate photosynthesis with this chemical equation:

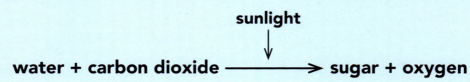

$$\text{water} + \text{carbon dioxide} \xrightarrow{\text{sunlight}} \text{sugar} + \text{oxygen}$$

As a result of photosynthesis, plants save some of the solar energy as sugar, which can be found in food molecules, such as starch in potatoes and rice. The molecules of oxygen are released into the atmosphere.

The Biology of Energy

Cellular Respiration

When an animal eats food, a three-stage process releases energy and makes it available to power cellular functions. As we know from Dr. Beaumont's studies, the first stage takes place outside of cells entirely. It is the work of the digestive system, which is made up of the mouth, esophagus, stomach, small intestine, and large intestine. During this first stage, the digestive system breaks

Fermentation

In order for cell respiration to occur, oxygen must be present. Sometimes, cells have to break down food molecules when oxygen is unavailable. They do this by using a different chemical pathway called fermentation. Interestingly, humans have adapted this to help us in many ways, particularly when it comes to food. Without even knowing it, we all probably eat something on a regular basis that exists due to fermentation.

The most familiar and practical applications of fermentation are the rising of bread and the production of beer and wine by yeast. Other microorganisms are responsible for making many other foods through fermentation: yogurt, pickles, sauerkraut, vinegar, Swiss and other types of cheese, soy sauce, and even chocolate.[2]

Biology in Your Everyday Life

apart proteins, carbohydrates, and fats into their simpler subunits. Food subunit molecules—amino acids, sugars, and fats—are rich in energy. The second and third stages, each with their own set of chemical reactions, then transform this energy into a form the body can use. These last two stages comprise cellular respiration, the process by which cells extract energy from food molecules. Stages two and three happen inside different areas within cells.

Transcription and Translation

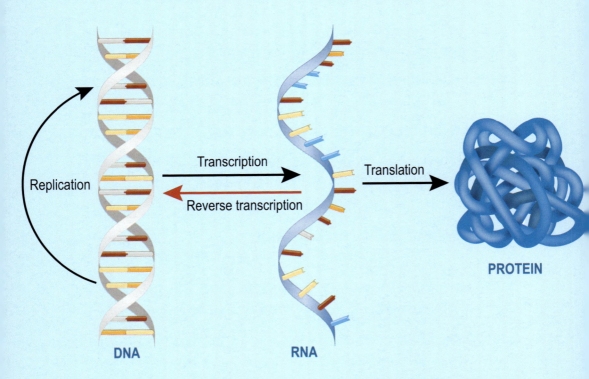

Cells use energy for biosynthesis in which molecules are joined together to make complex molecules such as the DNA, RNA, and proteins shown here.

Cellular respiration begins with energy-rich molecules, strips the energy from them, and transforms the energy so it can be used to support biological functions. It finishes with very low-energy waste products: carbon dioxide and water.

How Do Organisms Extract Energy?

In order to live a healthy life, organisms need to extract energy from their environments (sunlight or food) and use this energy to function. The breakdown of food molecules by cell respiration is called catabolism. Starting with energy-rich molecules, catabolism extracts this energy. In contrast, the production of complex structures is called biosynthesis. For example, joining amino acids together to make a protein is a biosynthetic reaction. Biosynthetic reactions require energy. The products of biosynthetic reactions have more energy than the starting materials. Humans and other organisms survive and thrive by balancing catabolism and biosynthesis successfully.

Activity: Do All Sweeteners Power Fermentation?

Test whether yeast, a single-celled organism, is able to ferment particular sweeteners. When yeast ferments, it makes the gas carbon dioxide, which will be easy for you to notice.

Things You Will Need:

- Baker's yeast
- Table sugar
- Splenda
- Sweet'n Low
- Equal
- Ziploc bags
- Heating pad

■ 1. Place one tablespoon of baker's yeast into each of four plastic Ziploc sandwich bags.

■ 2. Add one tablespoon of table sugar (sucrose) to one bag. Add one tablespoon of Splenda (sucralose) to another bag. Add one tablespoon of Sweet'n Low (saccharin) to a third bag. Finally, add a tablespoon of Equal (aspartame) to the last bag.

■ 3. Add 1/3 cup of warm water to each bag and seal the bags tightly, trying to get out as much air as possible. Mix the contents gently.

■ 4. Place the bags flat on a heating pad set on medium or high. Measure the heights of the bags.

■ 5. Measure the heights of the bags every ten minutes for the next thirty to forty minutes to see if carbon dioxide is collecting. Does yeast ferment certain sweeteners better than others? What types of sweeteners or other edible materials would make sense to test? Explain your thoughts.

The Biology of Human Differences

Chapter 5

Most of us know what it feels like to have a stomachache. For many people, stomachaches come and go; they aren't a regular part of everyday life. Others, however, are more susceptible to getting an upset stomach, particularly after eating a specific food. These stomach pains can be quite intense. People may experience intestinal cramping, bloating, diarrhea, and flatulence. Why do some people have negative reactions to certain foods while others can eat the very same things and feel just fine?

Dairy products, like cheese and ice cream, contain a sugar called lactose. Humans, just like all mammals, drink their mother's milk as infants, and most infants are able to break down lactose in breast milk. But the majority of humans lose this ability around two years of age. Worldwide, about 65 percent of us can't digest dairy products, and only 35 percent can eat foods that contain dairy, like ice cream and cheese pizza, without suffering uncomfortable side effects.[1] The inability to digest lactose varies in different regions of the world ranging from 10 percent in northern Europe to 95 percent in parts of Asia and Africa.[2]

Lactose is broken down by an enzyme called lactase. Enzymes are molecules that help cause chemical reactions. In most people, another gene shuts down lactase production after the age of two or so. In some people, however, there is a mutation, or change in DNA, that allows lactase production to continue on into adulthood. Because this mutation is not common around the world, most adults can't digest dairy products. Having said that, this mutation

Biology in Your Everyday Life

Sometimes, eating a food that a person cannot easily digest or break down can lead to a stomachache.

The Biology of Human Differences

is common in two groups of people: northern Europeans and their descendants and several ethnic groups from equatorial Africa. Using genetic techniques, scientists can estimate when this mutation first appeared. It became common in Europe about ten thousand years ago.[3] How can we explain the geographic distribution and age of this mutation?

There are many human characteristics that show geographic variation. These traits refer to those that occur in people in some places of the world but not others. Skin and eye color and the ability to digest alcohol are some examples of characteristics that relate to geographic variation. All of these traits are examples of

Dairy products include milk, cream, ice cream, butter, yogurt, and cheese.

Biology in Your Everyday Life

relatively recent human evolution that developed as our ancestors adapted to their local environments. In order to explain these variations, we must first understand evolution.

Evolution

Evolution, the theory that explains how all living organisms are related and how existing species adapt to their environments and new species arise, is the central unifying theme of biology.

Evolution helps us understand why biological processes work the way they do. Evolution also helps us understand many other important things about nature, like why organisms fit in so well with their environments, why so many species exist, and why some species are so similar while others are not.

Natural Selection

Natural selection is the mechanism that explains a great deal of evolution. Natural selection is based upon three facts observed in nature:

1. *Variation*: Individuals in a population of the same type of organisms vary; they differ from one another. For example, no two giraffes are identical.
2. *Inheritance*: Variations are inherited; when they reproduce, parents pass some of their variation on to their offspring.
3. *Differential Survival and Reproduction*: In any population of organisms, many more offspring are born than survive to adulthood. Although this is less the case for humans in most places in the world, it was certainly true for us earlier in our evolutionary history.

Certain individuals with particular variations would have a greater chance of survival and therefore a greater chance of reproducing. When they reproduced, these individuals would

The Biology of Human Differences

All organisms, including humans, evolved from earlier ancestors through the process of natural selection.

pass on to their offspring the variations that helped them survive. The next generation would have a higher number of organisms with those variable traits that improved the chances of survival and reproduction. Over time, a species would become better adapted to its environment. Scientists use the phrase "descent with modification" to describe the fact that species change—that is, they evolve.

Lactase and Human Evolution

Scientists have shown that mutations occur randomly. The particular mutation that allows lactase production to continue into adulthood has occurred many times throughout the 200,000-year history of our species,[4] and it has occurred across the world. But the mutation didn't "take," or become common in any

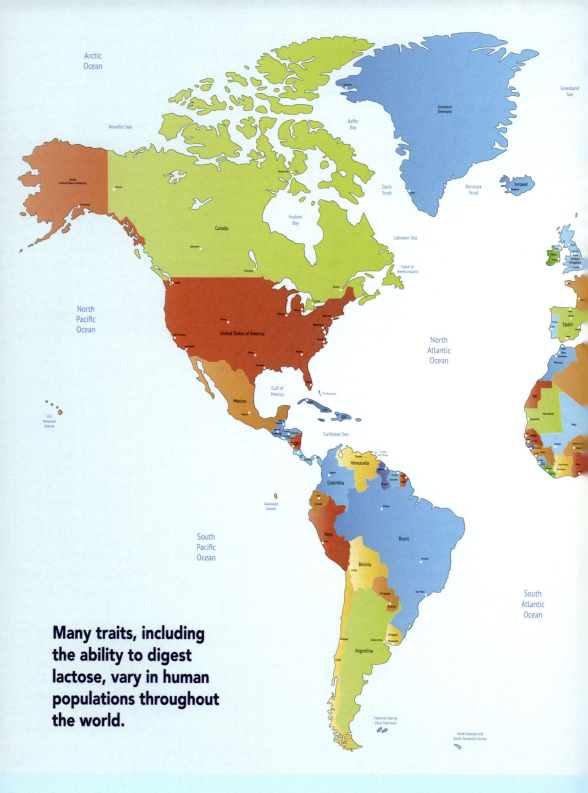

Many traits, including the ability to digest lactose, vary in human populations throughout the world.

Biology in Your Everyday Life

Why Do Bacteria Evolve Resistance to Antibiotics?

Eventually, every species exposed to antibiotics will evolve a form of resistance to these drugs. In fact, within two to ten years after a new antibiotic is introduced, new strains of disease-causing bacteria evolve that are resistant to it.[5]

Resistance evolves in a very simple manner. When you apply antibiotics to a population of bacteria, most of the cells are sensitive to the drug and they die. However, a few cells will survive. These cells will reproduce and form a population of resistant bacterial cells. This is an example of natural selection. Resistance evolves like any other trait. Environmental conditions favor some traits over others, and individuals with these traits become more common.

human population, until it occurred in northern Europe about ten thousand years ago. Why?

Consider what might happen to the mutation if it appeared in a typical settlement of our earliest ancestors. For an infant feeding on breast milk, lactase production is essential. But after the child is weaned from the breast, there is no more milk to drink. There are no domesticated dairy cows, no cheese, no butter, and no yogurt—nothing but meat, nuts, maybe berries, and other available plant material. Under these conditions, a mutation that allows adults to produce lactase would not provide any advantage. There would be no particular reason for the mutation to increase its frequency in the population.

This picture changes dramatically when domesticated cows and goats are around. Their milk provides a great food source for humans who can digest it. In times of food shortages—and there were plenty of those—an adult who could produce lactase might survive by drinking milk or eating other dairy products and could pass the mutation on to his or her offspring. An adult lacking the mutation might starve. Under these conditions, the mutation for lactase persistence would provide a key advantage and would likely become more common throughout a population that kept dairy animals.

A large group of dairy farms originated in northern Europe about ten thousand years ago.[6] Eventually the mutation for lactase persistence occurred in this population and became common. Among northern Europeans and their descendants in North America and Australia, almost all individuals can digest lactose as adults. The Tutsis and Fulanis of equatorial Africa also have many people in the population who continue to have functioning lactase and can therefore digest dairy foods. The Tutsis and Fulanis are also among the few African people who have a long history of herding dairy cattle. Adult-persistent lactase is an example of how natural selection acts on human populations and causes evolutionary change.

Activity: Natural Selection

You and your friends can pretend to be predators trying to catch prey (paper dots of different colors) and see natural selection in action.

Things You Will Need:

- **Patterned fabric**
- **Plastic cups**
- **Small dots made out of colored construction paper**

■ **1.** Grab a partner and piece of fabric. The fabric should be 3 feet by 3 feet (.9 meter by .9 meter) and have a complicated pattern with many colors. Put the piece of fabric on a flat surface.

■ **2.** Set up ten small cups, each containing one hundred construction paper dots made with a standard hole puncher. Each cup should have paper dots of one of the following colors: black, white, blue, red, yellow, purple, green, orange, pink, or brown.

■ **3.** One partner should randomly scatter ten dots of each color on to the multi-color cloth background. These dots represent a single type of organism that varies in color.

■ **4.** The other partner will collect dots, one at a time, until seventy-five have been collected. Record how many dots of each color were collected. The dots that were captured are "dead."

The Biology of Human Differences

■ **5.** Collect the twenty-five "surviving" dots. All of these dots are able to "reproduce" and make offspring. Place each surviving dot and three dots of the same color on the fabric to represent the reproduction of these survivors.

■ **6.** Repeat steps #4 and #5 four more times.

■ **7.** Do dots of a particular color survive better than others? Why?

Chapter 1
The Biology of Acne

1. RJ Hay, NE Johns, HC Williams, IW Bolliger, RP Dellavalle, DJ Margolis, R Marks, L Naldi, MA Weinstock, SK Wulf, C Michaud, C Murray, M Naghavi, "The Global Burden of Skin Disease in 2010: An Analysis of the Prevalence and Impact of Skin Conditions," *The Journal of Investigative Dermatology* 134 no. 6 (2013), p. 1527–34.
2. M Taylor, M Gonzalez, R Porter, "Pathways to inflammation: acne pathophysiology," *European Journal of Dermatology* (Review) 21 no. 3 (2011), p. 323–33.
3. "Acne," Mayo Clinic, https://www.mayoclinic.org/diseases-conditions/acne/diagnosis-treatment/drc-20368048 (accessed August 20, 2018).

Chapter 2
The Biology of Sexual Development

1. "Caster Semenya cleared to return to track immediately," Lipstick Alley, https://www.lipstickalley.com/threads/caster-semenya-cleared-to-return-to-track-immediately.243895/ (accessed August 20, 2018).
2. Anne Fausto-Sterling, *Sexing the Body* (New York, NY: Basic Books, 2000).
3. Ibid.
4. Barbara L. Drinkwater (ed.), *Women in Sport* (Oxford, England: Blackwell Science, 2000).
5. Robert Ritchie, John Reynard, and Tom Lewis, "Intersex and the Olympic Games," *Journal of the Royal Society of Medicine* 101 no. 8 (2008), p. 395–399.
6. "New IAAF testosterone rules could slow Caster Semenya by up to seven seconds," The Guardian, www.theguardian.com/sport/2018/apr/25/iaaf-testosterone-rules-caster-semenya (accessed August 20, 2018).

Chapter Notes

■ Chapter 3
The Biology of the Brain

1. "Concussion (Traumatic Brain Injury)," WebMD, https://www.webmd.com/brain/concussion-traumatic-brain-injury-symptoms-causes-treatments#2 (accessed August 20, 2018).
2. Ryan D'Agostino, "The Drugging of the American Boy," *Esquire*, March 27, 2014, https://www.esquire.com/news-politics/a32858/drugging-of-the-american-boy-0414/.
3. "Brain Facts that Make You Go "Hmmmmm," https://faculty.washington.edu/chudler/ffacts.html (accessed August 20, 2018).
4. "Brain," *National Geographic*, https://www.nationalgeographic.com/science/health-and-human-body/human-body/brain/ (accessed August 20, 2018).

■ Chapter 4
The Biology of Energy

1. Kat Eschner, "This Man's Gunshot Wound Gave Scientists a Window into Digestion," *Smithsonian.com*, June 6, 2017, https://www.smithsonianmag.com/smart-news/grisly-story-human-guinea-pig-alexis-st-martin-180963520/.
2. Monika Buzcek, "Chocolate: The Fermentation and the Flavors of the Chocomicrobiome," *Microbial Sciences*, March 30, 2017, https://www.asm.org/index.php/general-science-blog/item/6289-chocolate-the-fermentation-and-flavors-of-the-chocomicrobiome.

■ Chapter 5
The Biology of Human Differences

1. "Lactose Intolerance," Genetic Home Reference, https://ghr.nlm.nih.gov/condition/lactose-intolerance (August 20, 2018).
2. Y Deng, B Misselwitz, N Dai, M Fox, "Lactose Intolerance in Adults: Biological Mechanism and Dietary Management," *Nutrients* (Review) 7 no. 9 (2015), 8020–35.
3. Andrew Curry, "Archeology: The Milk Revolution," *Nature*, July 31, 2013, https://www.nature.com/news/archaeology-the-milk-revolution-1.13471.

4. Brian Resnick, "The Story of Human Evolution in Africa is Undergoing a Major Rewrite," *Vox*, Jul 3, 2017, https://www.vox.com/science-and-health/2017/6/7/15745714/nature-homo-sapien-remains-jebel-irhoud.
5. "About Antimicrobial Resistance," CDC, https://www.cdc.gov/drugresistance/about.html (accessed August 20, 2018).
6. K. Kris Hurst, "Lactose Intolerance and Lactase Persistence," *Thought Co.*, https://www.thoughtco.com/lactose-intolerance-and-lactase-persistence-170884.

Glossary

attention-deficit/hyperactivity disorder (ADHD) A commonly diagnosed mental issue that includes symptoms such as forgetfulness, impulsiveness, distractibility, fidgeting, and impatience.

biosynthesis Chemical reactions in cells in which simple molecules are put together to make more complicated molecules or structures, such as in photosynthesis.

catabolism Chemical reactions in cells in which energy-rich, complex molecules are broken down to extract energy, such as in cellular respiration.

cerebrum The largest part of the human brain, responsible for our reasoning ability, mathematical ability, artistic ability, imagination, language, and personality.

fermentation The process used by some cells, like yeast, to break down complex, energy-rich molecules when oxygen is not available for cellular respiration.

hair follicle A microscopic opening in skin from which hair grows.

lactase The enzyme that breaks down the sugar lactose.

limbic system Responsible for emotions, learning, memory, and physical drives, the limbic system is located in the forebrain.

Müllerian ducts During development, Müllerian ducts are present in both XX and XY embryos. If the appropriate instructions are received, the Müllerian ducts will develop into the internal parts of the female genital system.

natural selection The mechanism that explains evolution: organisms vary; some of this variability can be inherited; some variations improve the chance of survival and reproduction.

organ A group of tissues organized to make a structure that performs a specific function.

Biology in Your Everyday Life

testosterone A hormone or chemical signal made by both XX and XY individuals. Although it has many functions, testosterone is often associated with the development of male genitals.

tissue A group of cells attached to each other that carry out a particular function.

Wolffian ducts During development, Wolffian ducts are present in both XX and XY embryos. If the appropriate instructions are received, the Wolffian ducts will develop into internal parts of the male genital system.

Books

Becker, Jack, and Chris Hayhurst. *The Brain and Spinal Cord in 3D* (The Human Body in 3D). New York, NY: Rosen Publishing Group, 2016.

Cronn-Mills, Kirstin. *Transgender Lives: Complex Stories, Complex Voices*. Minneapolis, MN: Lerner Publishing Group, 2015.

Johnson, Rose. *Discoveries in Life Science that Changed the World* (Scientific Breakthroughs). New York, NY: Rosen Publishing Group, 2015.

Landon, Melissa. *Biology: Understanding Living Matter* (The Study of Science). New York, NY: Rosen Publishing Group, 2015.

Peterson, Judy Monroe. *I Have a Concussion, Now What?* (Teen Life 411). New York, NY: Rosen Publishing Group, 2017.

Randolph, Joanne. *Understanding the Brain* (The Amazing Human Body). New York, NY: Enslow Publishers, 2017.

Torres, John Albert. *Critical Perspectives on Minors Playing High-Contact Sports* (Analyzing the Issues). New York, NY: Enslow Publishers, 2018.

Zuchora-Walske, Christine. *Key Discoveries in Life Science*. Minneapolis, MN: Lerner Publishing Group, 2015.

Websites

Acne: A Visual Dictionary
www.webmd.com/skin-problems-and-treatments/acne/ss/slideshow-acne-dictionary
Look at different types of blemishes and learn about skincare and treatment.

Concussion
www.cdc.gov/traumaticbraininjury/symptoms.html
Read more about concussions, including symptoms, possible long-term effects, and prevention.

Metabolism
https://kidshealth.org/en/teens/metabolism.html
Check out how the human body gets energy from food and uses it for fuel.

Nervous System in Humans
https://www.hhmi.org/biointeractive/healthy-nervous-system-delicate-balance
Explore the structure and function of the nervous system in health and disease through this interactive site.

Sexual Development
https://kidshealth.org/en/parents/development-foyer.html
Get more information about puberty, reproductive systems, relationships, sex, and sexual orientation.

Index

A
acne, 4, 7-16
    activity, 15-16
    medications for, 7, 10-11
    myths, 12
    risk factors, 11-13
    treatments and
        preventions, 14
    types of, 9
antibiotics, 52
attention-deficit/hyperactivity
  disorder (ADHD), 16, 31

B
bacteria, 7, 10, 11, 52
Beaumont, Dr. William, 37
bioenergetics, 39
biology, 4-6, 48
biosynthesis, 43
brain, 28-36
    activity, 36
    parts of, 32, 34-35
brain injury, 4, 28, 31

C
carbon dioxide, 39, 40, 43
catabolism, 43

cells, 7, 8, 9, 11, 15, 20, 24, 31,
  39, 41, 42, 52
cellular respiration, 41-43
chromosomes, 20-21
concussion, 4, 28, 30, 32, 35

D
dairy, 45, 52, 53
digestion, 37

E
energy, 5, 37-44
    activity, 44
    cells, 39
    definition of, 39
    how it's extracted, 43
enzymes, 45
estrogen, 22, 24
evolution, 48
    human, 49, 52-53

F
fermentation, 41

G
geographic variation, 47

H
human differences, 45-55

63

Biology in Your Everyday Life

activity, 54–55
genetic techniques, 47
mutation, 45, 47, 49, 52–53
traits, 47–48

I

International Association of Athletics Foundation (IAAF), 17, 19, 26

L

lactase, 45, 49, 52–53
lactose, 45, 53
lactose intolerance, 5, 49–53
limbic system, 35

M

mental health, 31
molecules, 31, 39, 40, 41, 42, 43, 45
Müllerian ducts, 21–22, 24

N

natural selection, 48–49, 52, 53

O

organs, 7, 8, 9, 17, 21

P

photosynthesis, 39–40
physical health, 31
Propionibacterium acnes (*P. acnes*), 10–11
puberty, 12, 21, 22

S

Semenya, Caster, 17–19, 26
sex testing in sports, 25
sexual development, 4, 17–27
activity, 27
chromosome instructions, 21–22
hormone instructions, 22
formation, 19–20
stages of, 20–21
what happens, 24, 26
skin, 4, 7–9, 10, 12, 14, 47
SRY gene, 21, 24, 25
St. Martin, Alexis, 37

T

testosterone, 19, 22, 24, 26

W

Wolffian ducts, 21–22